The Matuschka Case

The Matuschka Case

Selected Poems 1970-2005

FRASER SUTHERLAND

We acknowledge the support of the Canada Council for the Arts
for our publishing program.
We also acknowledge support from the Ontario Arts Council.

Canada Council **Conseil des Arts**
for the Arts **du Canada**

ONTARIO ARTS COUNCIL
CONSEIL DES ARTS DE L'ONTARIO

Cover design by Heng Wee Tan

Library and Archives Canada Cataloguing in Publication

Sutherland, Fraser
        The Matuschka case : poems / Fraser Sutherland.

ISBN 1-894770-32-3

        I. Title.

PS8587.U79M38 2006   C811'.54   C2006-903025-1

Printed in Canada by Coach House Printing

TSAR Publications
P. O. Box 6996, Station A
Toronto, Ontario M5W 1X7
Canada

www.tsarbooks.com

CONTENTS

PREFACE

The selected poems that follow first appeared in periodicals, anthologies, and in my published books, with the exception of *Jonestown* (1996), a book-length poem whose structure does not lend itself to excerpting. For the same reason, I have tended not to include longer poems.

I like to believe that the poems represent the core of my poetic preoccupations over several decades, independent of dates of composition or publication. For this reason, I haven't hesitated to revise some poems; some will differ from the form in which they originally appeared. The poems are arranged in order of publication but I have not cluttered pages with bibliographic information, which may be found in the index at the end of the book.

Since these are published poems, the selections partly represent the taste of others, and thus are a useful check on my personal biases. I owe a debt to the editors and friends who first encountered them.

THE MATUSCHKA CASE

For some time now my hero has been Sylvestre Matuschka,
who could only get sexual satisfaction blowing up trains.
This interesting Hungarian blew up several
before he was finally captured, costing the railroads
a lot of money and killing quite a few people along the way.

The lesson to be learned from the Matuschka case, it seems to me,
is not the sexual satisfaction part of it,
(Unhappy Hungarian!), but rather this:
that here was that so very rare human being,
a man who truly knew what his pleasure was.

THE TRAIN MOVING

While they stand waving
we edge beyond where
their hands flutter,
bending at the wrists farewell
farewell, legs planted,
goodbye leaves growing
in their hair.

SOFIAN EPISODE

She has an infinite capacity
for scotch-and-water, his dollars are drained
are drained. Sofia Grand Hotel, spring, 1970.

She will change dollars into leva,
boredom into bed. Sofia is the capital
of Bulgaria.

She is a little on the plump side,
a lot on the plump side. Her scotch
gets mixed with his vodka. They invent a toast.

They talk in his bad, her better French. "*Je suis grec*",
watch the floor show, the jugglers,
the funny acrobats.

She tries English. "I know a very good place."
A very good place. They will go, go
to the very good place.

In the Sofia taxi his hand
meets a mixture of elastic and moist *fille*,
meeting and losing, soon they are there.

She has friends. Much clapping of hands
and close waltzes. The bar bill
is stupendous.

Over the jukebox. "Give me $20."
Une chambre privée, une chambre privée.
That's a private room.

They cannot go together, though, she must stay
a little while. The police are there,
the Sofian police are there.

Outside a second bar
she tries to reassure, says "Darling"
in thickly-scented Burglish.

In minutes she will meet him
at the Sofia Grand. The taxi driver
only speaks Bulgarian.

Our hero goes to wait for nothing
in front of the hotel, watching the smooth cobbles
of the square, clean as washed fleece.

THE PIAZZA

This is the turning
and this is the way down.
This is the avenue to the sea
by the pale colonnades
the dawnwind ruffling
the curtained seascaped day.

This is your happiness,
the wave-borne jests that lie
scattered on the tranquil sands,
these are veins in the marble,
the starfish found
outside its element.

This is de Chirico flesh,
the ruined king's last plaything,
this is something studied,
an effect, an overture,
these are the sand-roads
eternally made.

This is last night's burnished kiss.

UPSTAIRS WINDOW

Snow on the hillside, stipple-down
crisscross of snowflake, bands
of white on the ochre grass,
apple-tree netting
the grey translucent sky; all
is light yet this is dusk, down
the down downs and the uplands
curving to the blunt-tip trees
and the window frameline like
a Whistler panel divides me
from the ridge of fence, the neighbour's
farm and the snow is slanting down
to the last long boundaries
while the hills climb.

SIREN

Leaving her, it was always raining
in the morning darkness, sheets of rain,
leaves of the sky turning.

Waiting for the bus, I was amazed
at the bursting sky, the street
a waterfall,

and not thinking anything, just alone
wet and shivering, cramped
in a doorway, watching headlights

so I couldn't think of her
above me in her bed,
swimming in a sea, hers only.

⌒∞⌒

Or the time climbing the mountain
when days were like seasons
and pain was why

she lay on the dim bedsheet
behind drawn blinds, glucose ebbing
into veins that were also grey.

⌒∞⌒

And when she left, I didn't see the plane
rise into the haze, reaching for
the ocean. There was a long delay.

But coming back to find the rooms
she left behind her, empty now
without her, it was as if

someone pulled the plug
to leave me gulping:
a landed, stranded fish.

AUDEN'S FACE

Much of any poetry's dispensible, but
observe his face. A runic face, cracked
like baked clay, mud-veins left
by the drying sun. What are these hieroglyphics
this dry irony of skin? Read the message
of the temple broken open, the ark
desecrated. Was there ever a time better
than the one in which he lived? The sun
told him no. Bleached bones in a salt land
said don't forget us. Age limned
the parchment with memory, decay, life scored
the tablet vertical, horizontal. Writing words
carefully looked up, he sought precise truth, kept
life in one pocket, work in another
like pencils. This was Auden's face. He
chose, was given these serious ruins,
the mark of bitter weather.

BEGINNING

These are days when I would want to begin again
in some stranger-city, to drift into a bar
secretive and self-contained, my whole past
packed inside me like a bomb. An unknown
city, free of personal
associations. To begin again. To flower, each petal
full-looming in the light, until identified
as a common weed and then I
move on. To feel that lonely-aching hotel room
until I come to myself and strangely then
am grasped by others. To find new streets,
cafés, restaurants, and parks, a different soil,
to say, it's me, I'm here as indifference breaks
like a grey day's unexpected sun. *You don't know
about me I'm more than you think.*

WITH THE DOG

In the tenderness of rain we stroll,
the dog and I, not knowing where we go
though its parameter.
On cement indifference, through
poignant shrubbery, he pads or trots
instinctive to his truth.

We are alone,
though sometimes shapes emerge from mist
and then recede. He stays
on the leash of my eyelid.
We are happy, the dog and I,
in this climate of corners.
He makes his mark, discovers
that of others, I leave my traces too.

His nose is to the ground,
the upturned earth, and the tempo of the rain.
Coming home, we pause at the traffic light,
are met at the door by the two cats,
who somehow seem onlookers
like shrubs in the erasing rain.

GOOD TIMES

Tell me about the old times, the good times,
what were they like?
When oranges were green and sweet, speckled with orange
as oranges should be
and one could actually touch her skin,
not collide with hard impacted flesh.
Tell me about the good times

tell me about the times when you felt bodiless
in the warm consoling air.
Lights in water were your harvest home,
the moon a pumpkin, hands moist earth,
promise was the name of the quiet country night,

tell me about the white wine in the beaded pitcher
the street acrobat swallowing a cigarette,
tell me about something that happened,
could not recur, a splinter of happiness,

tell me about her mist-grey eyes, call them seas,
call them seasons, take me down the lilting road
to the old times, to the memory
of what I never had.

Today penicillin and a big cigar.

CITY MEN

The city is a wound, we are its blood
streaming in a livid dream of pain.
Monoxide stings the eye and no tree wakes us
as we walk toward the nearest citadel in
which controlled airs wait for us.

                              Then shall we
take flight to a pastoral of innocent lakes?
They want that highway now and
snowmobiles will run you ragged.
Dead buildings stare, their boarded windows
hit on the blind side, shall soon
be disinherited.

                        The city dreams us all.
Awaiting some announcement of the dawn,
the furniture trembles at sinister vibrations.
I hear the distant hellish machinery
rumbling overnight; a refrigerator, too, adds
its infernal hum.

                              At 4:51 a.m.
light starts behind my eyelids,
battalions spreading over the basalt city,
each leaf a salute, the light a population,
tonsure of pain like a shrapnel wound.

                              Tribal fires go out
and violent dawns crash down on us,
tunnels of sun and wind where people spin
like pollen and clay pigeons climb
the churning air. The
mad spring makes us madder,
spokes of a giant wheel begging
us still to be gentle, still to be good.
But we are city men, hate
our poison and cannot do without it.

14

ON FOREIGN WOMEN

You ask me why I'm attracted to foreign women
and I'll try to put the matter simply.

Foreign women never ask questions,
they have all the answers.
Foreign women are flexible
because they're used to invasions,
they're good in bed because they have
centuries of breeding.

Foreign women have tact.
I'd let a foreign woman poison me.

Foreign women are women
but they have an extra something:
I think it's their charming accent.

Foreign women are intelligent.
For a foreign woman even a Hollywood film
has sub-titles.

Foreign women, if they have problems,
have *interesting* problems
and maintain superiority
over their psychiatrists.

Foreign women are good travellers.
She'll put her head on your shoulder.

ATTRACTION

Your bruised mouth, the end of seasons,
compels me more than simple reasons,

your cut breath is more a cue
than psychiatry's feeble clue

and when I take your hand that bleeds
it satisfies all my needs.

In each of these I find the name
of that murdered hole from which I came.

MADWOMEN

Madwomen ask to be legendized.
The long muscles of their thighs Madonna-smooth for kisses,
their painters' hands range our faces for hints of change,
they lock their legs to ours, molecular cement, holding patterns
while they stalk the high pavilions then drift
among orgasmic clouds and gonorrheal legacies:
nightshadows and nightmusic, ciphers, cadence, integers
lusting for completion. And we disperse ourselves in glints,
rapid to their shuddering, shallow to their depth,
the tunnel and the well.

They have come from their caves
to lope across the moonstruck fields, coasting in translucence,
silent hunters of a god to cleave
their land's bright furrow. They demand
to be made madder, bullet-riddled with enigmas,
born again to night's synaptic thrillers, the touch
that makes them one with their own moans, each
a stranger animal, a keening Magdalene writhing for
the probing finger deep within the wound.

Closer to wind and hell and the godhead than you or I
they are wind-streaked water or butterflies like flames
imploring the poison-bottle and the mesh, riveted bones,
pinned wings, to be told what they are. Yet madwomen break free,
hungry as Bacchae, their manes lashing astonished air,
wild mares in a season of storms. Then they are mild,
nuzzling sugar. "Tame me, tame me," they say.
But it's a lie. The truth was St. Teresa who, yowling like a cat,
slavered for the Lord in sacred rut—
a crack of lightning beckoning the thunderbolt
she aimed to be immortalized any way she could.

PHONING

Sometimes I even forget it's a phone,
it's so much like whispering in an ear.
I like to hold my breath, and then exhale.
At first they hang up, or disconnect,
but then they get hysterical: that's what
I like the best. One woman sobbed,
she would have kept it up for hours
but I got sick of her whimpering.
I find them in the phone book: single
initials are the likeliest; by hearing voices
I can figure out if they're working girls,
divorcées, young widows if I'm lucky.

                              I think of them
breathless by the phone, hearing me.
Sometimes I lay on a little catch.
I hear them gasp at the other end
and sometimes I almost pant
to get reactions. I'm good at it. I don't
check up on them, anything like that.
Jesus no I don't want to ever
meet them, I just want to hear them cry.

BONES

I knew a woman, know her now, will know her
when bones walk on that last day.
Her bones talk to me, they speak
of rest, and swim beneath the skin.
I bend them but they will not break
nor stretch - bones cannot suffer harm.
The grinning teeth pull taut
the veil of colour, filament of hair,
say this is life and living now, so
kiss the lovely mask. Bones know,
waiting for their long dry future,
that death is not the outcome, for
bones cannot lie. The hair goes grey, wrinkles
are traitor cells, but bones go on
though they be brittle. Bones in my hand,
a basket for your heart, the temple
of the brain, the vertebrae on which I play
motets, bones of your body in the wind
where we walk on that last day.

AGAINST THE REASONING MIND

You rimmed the moistened lip with salt,
the glass turning in your hand.
The words run down,
richer than poison, noiseless
and patient, perfect as some prayers.

You have slept, a mind pitching toward
some hole that cannot be identified.
You have walked to an orchard, picked an apple,
offered it to me,
the white and swarming life,
the busy wound. Mystic animal,

how many times have we slept together?
Three hundred, a thousand times?
I have walked to the corner store,
the air replete with pleading,
walked down the street, bled
by the moon's slow autopsy.

My desire's become relentlessly abstract,
it would be ruined by a whisper, a word.
The inside of a thigh's not so much touched
as left.

Against the reasoning mind
the world made random. Birds and ash.
I'll be anything you will.
With any portable probable myth, victory with
a dead battery I'll be
your saturnine lizard swimming in eros,
your roaring boy.

Once again a finger to the gash
I'll stroke the pretty wound, living out the dream's
rough mercies, country justice,
bring you today this little death.

How signs, words, acts, dreams
sift into silt, shift into stone,
words in water, white on white skin, phlegm on snow.
Nothing takes me back to where it started,
the last whisper.
The heartbeat on my wrist says three o'clock.

IN THE PROVINCES

The chapped lives of small-town girls
shed successive skins of purity.
What do you expect?
It's how it's done in the provinces.

The teeth of the neighbour's kid
could peck corn through a screen door
but just the same there are some awful pretty girls
driving trucks in the provinces.

In places called the Coffee Pot
the boys order a hot waitress to go
and lives reach out in an endless ellipse.

The watched girls thread by on spindles.
Do their nights flare with the cupped flame
of a man simply pausing, lighting up? Or does
it all end on a road in ruts back of the golf course?

Farmers regularly drive their cars down embankments.
It's a way of making sure of a new car every year
and how they tell if you're any good in the provinces.

The big cities look down on the little cities.
The little cities look down on the towns.
The towns look down on the country
and some people in the big cities
want to move to the country
because they think there's something good in the provinces.

The old folks aren't after a fast buck.
They look for moral triumphs,
are obsessed with weather and funerals,
or dispossessed.

The kids commute two hours a day
to modular blocks that get bigger and smaller,
wave good-bye to the old folks' motel
bigger and smaller, awaiting some news.

Some parts want to split away
and some parts want to stay
but it's all the same in the provinces.

I once worked for a parrot-beaked limey jerk
and a bum steer of a Scotsman, his underling.
They came from the provinces
to fart for pay in Canada.
Such men in groups are dangerous.

The seas are slick with oil
from TV production crews
who film each other drilling,
the rancid pulp mills
poison the veins of earth
for mines go deep in the provinces
and all the commercials are made there.

In a clever public relations move Scott Paper
has hacked out cross-country ski trails
but one of these days they'll spray skiers,
confusing them with the spruce budworm,
then they'll have to re-schedule
because the Book of Ecclesiastes was written in the provinces
though a time to die is everywhere.

The player-piano winds say not much here
but the disco-bomp of bouncing snowmobiles
which search for fine days, deep snow, and shell ice.
Rabbit snares offer a grammar of these woods,
the blood-lust of indifference.
The curb-kissed city kid, the man hunting coons in the corn,
are brother provincials, hooked on death,
smear on the snare.

You think the whales are in troubles?
In Africa the elephant poachers are spiking bananas
with battery acid.
They want to clear the earth of the damned things.
We need more paved roads in the provinces.

I will try to learn the language of the provinces.
I speak it imperfectly.
No one's ever said the name of the subtle desolation
in a road crew's back road half-built house,
nor has anyone ever plumbed
the infinite cruddiness of a Loew's Hotel.

OLD N.S.

Here people stay the same. They don't bend,
alter, shift, or move perceptibly.
They're somewhere in behind the landscape,
hiding back of trees. They only come out
when the white light of Progress beams
upon them. Then they're etched sharply.
Sometimes they're seen
flitting from blackened stump to stump,
seeking cover. They become what people
tell them, yet stay stubbornly
the same. Moving away, you're a strange
native son, remaining, stranger still.
The softness comes after the salt,
highways meld with logging trails,
you meet folks, are yourself embarrassed,
slightly flustered at your knowledge of them, of
yourself. This is one sea-road. The rest
is stark raving reality.

"VISAGES DANS LA RUE"

— Jules Supervielle

These faces in the street, how can we know them,
how can we think we know them?
Why can we never have a surfeit
of such faces, why do they pursue us?
Eyes changeable blue, flecked jade,
Chinese black like painted porcelain,
making us want to swim or sink half-struggling,
looks languorous, pleurant take responsibility
for words turned, tasted
in each station of the Metro
on the border of the dream.

How beautiful in sleep they are, these passengers,
how kind their mouths' tender entrances
a breathing quiet darkness.
They sleep, unmoved by God's enormities,
with the cowardice and dignity of death.
Like castaways they cling, but to a thread
that keeps them stitched in life's design.
They breathe, but do they live?
Slumped mannequins in a silent wake,
mourning their days, mourning their own death.

Montréal lies adjacent to the border of the dream.

TRACES

Beyond particulate she waits,
this loyalty to an old idea,
these almond eyes the slots of chance
this soul a dredge drawing up sediment
of dreams, racial memory, ancestors
who may have been Chinese,
woven fingers on a jar.
My fingers now reach across centuries
to clutch the note, bar, phrase
while dolphins flourish,
the blue flute beyond my depth.

Let me hold, like a bunch of heavy lilacs,
the evening's colour.
If a flower had a will it might renew its petal,
or ink, its stain.
And this, anonymously lovely,
might be mine.

                 ⌒∞⌒

At the back of a book she was written her name
in Chinese characters. On a scrap of paper
her telephone number—a bobby-pin, a hair
in the bath remind me that
she has been here, traces of a ruined civilization,
persuading me one night was long enough
to include the now in which I perish,
a stencil upon time, as museum walls
are crowded with the wary living.
My days are huddled to her; she
has left her text on me,
the macrocosmic particle whose finger traces
silhouette-facsimile, in air the very likeness.

                 ⌒∞⌒

Someday a sign with be enough, a mark, a stroke
caligrammatic. I will not suffer,
will not have to live
that startled joy a first slow entry
as statues come into their being.
I will not have to taste, be lonely or ecstatic,
will not have to catch the train
or to wait and welcome home a friend.
I will not have to tend the garden
but find a forest in a weave of paper,
storms in the still bottle. I will be satisfied.
One stroke, a sign, a mark across the white page
will be enough. As in a Chinese wall-painting
someday like those flamingos I will fly
straight to the hieroglyphic
as clouds trail the branch.

ONLY MY TYPEWRITER

against the hysterical pregnancies
of Canadian female novelists,
the cigar store Indians
of Canadian male novelists.

Rides the wave
of a keyboard balance,
pulls me from drowning.

Weathers the weather,
succeeds in murder,
keeps me on time.

Rain on the windowsill
like horses cantering on cobblestones.
Only my typewriter talks back.

I knew a woman well.
The well is deep.
Only my typewriter says,
Write about it.

It's good to sleep with someone you care about,
to get drunk happily with friends,
to eat one's fill in a cosy café—
to find these things, and sometimes to travel
the airport avenue to a new place.
But only my typewriter pleads,
Come back to me.

Only my typewriter
warms me in winter,
woos the white morning.

LOVING

These days people make distinctions
between "loving" and being "in love."
It would seem "loving" is a sort of senility
but being "in love" is all hotsy-totsy.

Passionate women, why not tell me
how to feel while you're at it.
Give me a script. I'm only
your mirror anyway, your echo.

If you want to use diction I don't understand
you're entitled to and
have lots of company. For me, though
such currency is counterfeit.

Love shines in every toothpaste ad.
Hate would be more honest if only half the truth.
The other half is rage. My lexicon is missing
the loving page.

SOME CASES IN POINT

A poet tells how he once lived with a girl
and in the summer moths would fly into the house,
flutter everywhere. After bitter arguments
the girl would go running naked and crying,
turn her face to the wall—like a moth.

Machado says of *nunca, nada, nadie,*
the most terrible is *nadie.* No one.
Nothing, personified.
Always never.
Never to be understood. No one there.

The air's a tunnel of tumbling snowflakes
under the slate ceiling.
Thus night involves the sky
and the hard rind of cold
contains such flickering fruits.

ENTRY IN A DIARY

18 September 1975

The more grey matter, the more animals grow resigned
to death, it's said, the tired dolphin
heads for the net. Last night this tired animal
spurned two attractive females to get
incapably drunk, puke on the carpet, cut his hand
on a broken beer bottle
and sleep on the floor of a friendly acquaintance.
In the morning he rose quickly and restored
his heart with caffeine and codeine
and had all day the most extraordinary sense
of well-being, as if unwittingly
he'd strayed into a life.

ALLONS VOIR SI LA ROSE

— Ronsard

And does the rose
bloom in its accustomed place,
the green at the heart of the rose?

The lilac is full of summer.
Blue, you think of sky,
its pages opened by swallows.

The ripe apple leaps from the bough.
Its seeds taste of almond.
Ash Wednesday, chill water in clay.

New oats and new barley, green, greener,
the wind, hands in their hair
their secret sonata, like fear

the deer have come to the orchard,
cropping at apples. They sweetly crouch
on frozen ground.

The colt and the yearling plunge
in the first moist wind,
kick high into summer.

Go see if the trillium
blooms in the snow. Frost flowers.
White. White. White.

The wild rose and the white rose
within their hearts
discovered green.

THE MAN WHO HEARD SYMPHONIES

Sometimes he surrendered to that powerful surge,
symphonic bell curve, a gulf of notes,
desiring to be lost in its pulsive thunder,
germinating migraines counted through their cycle
metronomic pain slowing into sleep. He once
studied engineering but took up sketching
rugged chairs and houses, objects regulated
to intricate geometries of near meridians,
interested in the hermeneutics of canals and locks,
homeostasis. His mind reflexive, his suction
ejected our words like bent coins, on occasion
was moved to the salt of tears. His eyes, magpie-tragic,
plucked odd dictionary words, inverse multiples
of lopsided logarithms. He was puzzled
these wouldn't do as cogs in a machine.
The dark pupil was studying perfection.
He was always realistic! We spurned his wreck-beach
of aboriginal calamity, our dives mere paddling
not contests with submerged tidal rivers.
Or we tottered near the edge, drew back.
preferring not to fall. Here was a man who
wanted to be paterfamilias
as he faced a body count of scribbled integers.
He was more hermetic than we thought,
left with the water-fatal music, mounting
the staggered staircase to new levels.
Yet we cannot leave him there, or if we do,
it must be among continuing enterprises
alien to the less inventive. At last report
he was composing totems with a chainsaw.

"NOW IS THE TIME
TO HOLD HER CLOSE AND TELL HER YOU LOVE HER"

— from a sex manual

Now is the time when wolves howl in the cornfields.
The atomic night becomes a chrysalis.
Night slides in like a sliver into flesh.
The forest edge retreats to bedlam.

Now is the time of the hawk on the hydro line.
So we are married, grating rapture's
tonnage of the instants' change.
Bricks unravel, leaving home.

The gun sights on a long possibility.
Death stares down the creation myth.
Now is the time of breakage and mourning,
foliage in the magnesium flare.

Now is the time of amputations
whistling to the embarking sweat,
three silences, deadliest,
you and I and the other.

Windows on the canal.
Sentries in the street.
Humaine trop humaine,
the time of unleashing

beauties into a far corner
winding up the immortal simper,
the God who comes and goes away.
Refugees flee the gradual bomb,

sifting to clear air,
static as stitches,
as dissolving,
suturing calm.

Notes are spinning
pianissimo,
your bell of hair like blood
ceaselessly streaming.

The Northern Lights inflect the void.
Language queers our steadiness.
In the appalling drift
clouds are seeding our quietness.

RETURN TO COLD COMFORT FARM

I awoke this morning to a solitary chainsaw
cracking and ripping the country air.
The chain-fangs tore and bit at the first
of a row of Russets, said to be wormy
and going at the core. He bucks to the leaning blade
that embarks like a killer. A city man born
on this stony peninsula I have no clear answer
to my father's swooping saw, to
the denial of the old by the old,
to this cleared ground.
Nor can my powers of survival
enclose the ways of barbarous settlement
and everything up to date.
Wandering home at intervals I
have gained a costly freedom,
not learned that on this hill in Nova Scotia
all things come to be accepted,
a three-headed calf, a parking lot.

THE BLOOD-ORANGE MOON

A lonely hanging sun, the moon is full of itself.
In Bethel Cemetery, the corpses take their Sunday stroll,
Why should we living wake?

In the several darknesses the leaves are fronds,
oarmen of the outer river.
Our lives are cryptocrystalline.

But we have more neighbours than we thought
in the opaque passages.
They are making deliveries. Calling cards.

Yet that moon, a rutted pippin,
a swollen bitter tangerine,
is picked out of darkness.

WHITEFACES

Time to fathom the ineffable boredom,
chromatic ennui of whitefaces.
Walking downtown, one sometimes sees
black or yellow or red, but
in town whitefaced librarians stamp books,
white merchants sell skim-milk merchandise.
If I, a whiteface, am bored,
think of the depthless boredom a blackface
feels enveloped by white.

Around here even hitch-hikers.
Never seen a black hitch-hiker.
No one would pick him up,
afraid of dark odours inside the car.
One thing might lead to another,
a blackface coming home to supper,
asking for a second helping, a blackface
dating your whey-faced daughter,
a blackface taking your job,
raping your wife, crapping in your garden,
borrowing sugar, dunning you for rent,
boll weevils in the oatmeal, famine
and pestilence, the common cold.

The drama group to which I belong.
Same thing. Whitefaces
boring as Charolais or chalk pits.
I come from a long bleached line of Scots,
Calvinists before Calvin.
Think of South Africa: black, coloured, colourless
Or think of this village: whitefaces
buying groceries, whitefaces
breathing heavily through whitemasks.
making one sympathize with renegade girls
who take on big stupid bucks.
The worst of them could not be so boring
as my neighbour, the Hereford steer across the road.

The vanilla people grudgingly buy chocolate.
Only on television does a blackface appear
and then as a visitor from another planet,
The Third World. After watching him,
the whitecouple repairs to whitesheets
for a ghastly copulation.
How can they sleep in the dark?
They add bleach to their wash.
They are 99 44/100 per cent pure.
The weather report says snow tomorrow.
Again I will be blinded in the arctic glare,
and though I hide my face behind dark hair
some mornings I cannot bear to look
at the whiteface in the mirror.

FORMS OF LOSS

Begin with a button off your best shirt.
Or: your mate, car, children
born and unborn. Someone steals your luggage,
a kind of rape. The first time is the worst.
Then later it seems you're better off without
freedom, but then freedom is illusion
so we're back with what we started,
to love, honour, and cherish
the end, the void that turns questions into answers.
Some day we will find ourselves there,
someone else's lost enquiry.

Is there anything more than leaving and losing,
parting and packing,
framing the last photograph?
When we came it was to move and remove,
so also when we went.
Where the picture hung
is now a nail in the plaster.
That, too, is a picture.

Loss is given us, and we take it.

IN THE WHITE MORNING

The white morning waves,
warns, it waits.
Westward, the sun's parabola
has come this way with snow
fallen in the night.

The hills are pruned by a white gardener.
The trees have also bloomed
strong cold flowers: each
as cold as the pine boards
yet warmed by the permissive sun.

The house, then, is a landscape
brought home. The chimney a clumped branch
for the flickering prose of a bird
whose rest is a paragraph.
We do not hear

the breathing of this world
though it goes on
to issue a mark like a footprint.
We do not touch the cold
yet its cleansed reach is everywhere.

A bare table in a bare room,
a sheet of white paper,
white china cup and saucer.
Words like algebra
or the filigree window.

EZRA POUND
AND MY LATE UNCLE ORVILLE DUSENBERRY

A steady diet of corn produces the Turkey-wattled Opinionator.
Ezra Pound and Orville Dusenberry were of that breed.
I wish you could have heard my late Uncle Orville
on race and politics. Though you didn't have to.
You can read Ezra Pound.

Fate had given their views unequal exposure.
You may read the annotated verdicts of Pound
solemnly weighed, dignified by footnotes,
but Uncle Orville's remarks were silenced by spadefuls of earth
in St. Petersburg, Florida.

From that six-foot depth Uncle Orville no longer observes
"If Lincoln had lived he woulda put the nigras on reservations."
The "nigras", like Ezra's "jews", commanded his attention.
Nigras won prizefights because of thick craniums,
handy for butting.

Orville was, among other things, a barber. "I cut," he told me,
"lotsa black men's hairs." His politics condemned
fellow Missourian Harry Truman. "Truman was a profane man."
(Remember, Pound couldn't stomach Roosevelt, who declined
his monetary counsel.)

Orville Dusenberry drove a long low car, married twice,
the second wife being my Aunt Jo. For a time
he made the Massachusetts spinster happy, as Pound
is said to have summoned the devotion of his womenfolk,
for a while at least.

Pound and Dusenberry were both mulish men, holding fast
to credos, unrepentant in later life. It's true that Orville
was never committed to a cage for treason, nor was
he given a Roman microphone to broadcast his wide-ranging ideas,
that's a fact,

though in Orville's case I'd say it was respectively
a miscarriage of justice and a grace of God. I can still see
his Adam's apple working up the juice of words,
chomping at truth; Pound's lean ranting silhouette
still afflicts me.

They were so sure of everything. Though, near the end, my uncle
went off his head screaming mad and Ezra lapsed into frailness,
in only two significant ways do the men differ.
My late Uncle Orville Dusenberry knew fewer languages
and Ezra Pound had more talent.

GEORG TRAKL VISITS
CHAFFEY'S LOCKS, ONTARIO, ONE DAY IN FALL

The radiant hamlet was dying in images of brown.
Trakl looked for his sister,
heard her murmur among dank foliage.
She'd fallen in the lake last winter,
glazed the locks with a silver corruption,
ivory mask for this stonetree country
of nightsong, birdsleep.
This was his land for sure,
lost and sick and silent,
brackish water bidding muteness,
in the goldrip maples sundered angels,
their leaves bleeding bread.
Stripped trunks were purifying agony,
agonizing purity. His host—
perhaps he was Christ, or a ghost—
set off wielding chainsaw.
His host's father was a doctor
sunk in a dark secret. He'd once refused
medication to a barnful of the dying.
Under the moon Trakl was led to a grove
with crowns of leaves like morganatic marriages
or a head count of starving refugees.
Hanged bodies swung speechlessly
from broken elms. Down the blank road
people kept goats in a stripped orchard.
The goats were taking ominous lunch.

COLD HOUSE

Big cold house with a buffalo chair,
horns bound with rawhide straps like a torture instrument.
But torture would be something animate,
a scream in childbirth, fecund.

Here lived my pompous kindly uncle
with his frigid horror of a wife.
The verdigris teeth of my relative by marriage
juts like a sore on her savage lips.

Why did they marry?
Were they the only college graduates around
and hence must mate?
Suspecting pregnancy, she said,
"If I am, he'll pay for it."

She wasn't, but he paid anyway.
He let a business partner rob him
Why move or change?
A gentle sarcastic man resigned to one blind eye,
his dingy little town,

once he took me downtown to eat
after she dumped our veal chops on the lawn.
She gave him a stroke. He lay paralyzed and silly.
He died and didn't leave a will.
He never had one.

Sloppy lord of the beer rings
on Canadian Legion tables,
he had his triumph there,
to pronounce correctly,
to ask for "a good cigarette."

In their courting days they exchanged love letters.
For a Legion banquet he put a rose in his lapel.
She snarled, "Not appropriate."
Perhaps it wasn't.

SELF-CONSUMED

In the red persuasion of stretched skin,
the thudding flesh, we feel
sweat's power on the epidermis,
salt and soil and suede. Ambidextrous,
double-jointed, febrile as a yogi,
we strain to prove a point. That glow
pounds it home. Lips surround the glans,
drawing from the succulent bulb
a white flower, or hoping to.

Arms surround ourselves, we are going
deeper, our tongue recedes, the
cave encloses the explorer hardened
for an unspeakable penetration, who
will go plunging on and on
in hope of the more receptive mouth.

༺∞༻

What is this face
face down in the mirror?
Whose body mirroring mine?
Where tends this joining, this membership?

When will this trickling, swelling, gorging end?
Why does the white fluid
pool on the skin? Which man
is he who holds me in his two brown arms?
Have we met?

ANATOMIE

Pale limbs. Dark eyes.
A car cleaves the traffic,
the river skies.

The night climbs
to meet the day,
a wrist jumps, a spark

lighting leopard shoulders.
Fingers make a treaty
with her hair.

Her waist an apostle
pleading peace,
alliance française.

❧

Let her blood be a river.
Let her lips be a chain.
Let her mouth be an anchor.

❧

How the skin dreams
of what it lost,
walking away.

EDEN

1.

There in the swathing cosy silence
we will live. Abundance of blankets
piled in the closet. Fireplace heat
swimming on your face. Sometimes,
just for the cold of the thing, we'll step
into the night black as the moon's far half
while the stars wink immoderately.
Back inside, I'll read Yeats,
undisturbed by humming of the bees.
At last, yawning at each other,
we'll go upstairs and fuck exquisitely
while snow cocoons the cabin.

2.

Then spring will come. We'll stand
by the tumbling brook and watch twigs
spinning in the melted snow. We'll dig
slush canals, dams, bridges, aqueducts,
laughing, splashing. When the weather warms
I'll pretend to set out the garden
but you'll do all the work. Your cooking
is divine: the hodge-podge in the pot
murmurs new peas, tiny onions. Butter bubbles
on my plate. We eat damn well and
cheerfully curse the June bugs.
I can't wait to swim in the lake.

3.

Suddenly summer. I see you wading
in the shallows, the sun on your freckled skin
Once in a while I drift to the village
to pick up the mail. It's a cheque
for the last novel. They want photos.

I tell them to look in my file.
That afternoon we go after raspberries—
a black bear shambles across our path,
nods agreeably. Our pails brim.
Tipped into bowls, berries blend
with cream from the cool dark larder.

4.

The leaves turn but everything stays
the same between us. The rat-tat
of my typewriter is muffled by the pinewood
door. I'm writing the best of my life;
through the window see you prod
a mound of leaves. Where do
you walk this crunching day?
Soon you'll be with me; my lips
on the nape of our happiness.
The Fall is no fall for us. We live
on a plateau as we tell each other
that we have never known some other.

LEAMINGTON CEMETERY

is just past the town of Springhill
whose Institute resembles from the road
a barracks, base camp, pumping station,
or experimental farm, a think tank
to those inside who practice self-sufficiency
in the damp air of March,
serving time.

Townsmen were bumped too often
among the hard coal seams,
the maze of grimy beds,
so a government built this labyrinth
of watchers and the watched.
Medium security
for the unemployed.

The cemetery has had a recent burial,
a mound of earth, toppled plastic baskets
spilled roses still fresh.
No name makes an announcement,
only the 23rd Psalm's
"Lord is my shepherd. . ."
In the chilly dusk a dog barks.

The gravestones offer a wealth of Hunters.
Abram A. & Gladys J.
whose disastrous years
are marked by conical stones
among them three tiny ones
like fingers toes
        Baby Baby Baby
in the harrowed landscape,
silent beneath tramping boots
of killing time.

It seems that time itself's the Hunter.
buried here but going on.

That time's the god not so much to worship
as to obey.
That time will tell, as my late uncle said,
now buried in a plot not unlike these.
That time blooms into stones.

In minutes I will visit men
under sentence of temporary death.
In hours I will leave them
to their narrow graves
behind provisional cement.
Other men will close the door on them
while I go free into my own time.

THREE FEMININE FANTASIES

I. *Power*

She would like to arrange everything.
Assignations are plotted months ahead,
intricate planning prepares the way.
She has foreseen the time when she
and her lover outgrow this relationship,
phase into another.
By then she'll have found the perfect girl for him.
She knows him better than he knows himself.
He will be grateful.
She has put aside writing plays.
Why bother writing for professionals
when amateurs are so enthusiastic
and readily cast themselves in roles?
Certainly her husband is predictable.
She knows that if she should die
he'd cut his work adrift to drink
in hotel bars the wide world over,
sorrowing. Her sons' choice of wives
has not always been as she wished,
nonetheless a challenge to stagecraft.
Her scheme is to make them happy and whole,
worshipping with separate steps
her careful plan. In their own children,
in the talents of her lovers she'll live on,
subtly powerful.

II. *Dissolution*

To be held forever is her desire.
He will be she and himself, she
will be he and herself, the four
of them complete.
Sensations pouring light
melt resisting flesh,
all claims thereby reconciled.

In the curves and currents of earth
she and her lover will be earth.
They'll be the fresh breeze
from the ocean, be
the smell of summer sun on skin,
unified and omnicellular,.
Best of all, shall form the formless sea.
The last part of herself's a fish
swimming within these tides until
she is no longer she.
The sea takes over
and caressing water flows, lovely and inexorable
yet no one knows its name.

III. *Felicity*

Happiest performing.
Paint her a picture, any picture,
then put her at the centre,
the most conspicuous caryatid
or the centaur's favourite nymph.
She's not married, partly because
the role lacks variety.

Call her Ephigenia.
She gives herself for the good of her father's ships.
In a "holy time as quiet as a Nun"
she is the most devoted sister,
though a pair of flashing eyes
are the pincers of surprise.

She should be Mary
because Mary is so many things.
Massaging the feet of her Lord
or giving birth to Him
or going and sinning no more
or keening prostrate at the Cross.
Any decent painter prefers her to the Saviour.

She likes to complete people's sentences
because she can't be sure

they won't make a botch of it.
In dramatic pieces for two persons
she grants first place to another.
An intelligent audience accepts
that the important figure is herself.

Yet she's not in it for the glory:
quiet acclaim will be enough,
caring fingers across her fur.
She will gratefully peck at crumbs,
happiness an open palm;
loving: felicity.

HERE

I. *Driving Back*

Each pit, each pockmark of the road.
The shapes of night,
companionship.
The branches wave goodbye.

We have travelled great distances
inside each other's bodies,
slumped in the half-light
a headless rider.

Once the engine kicked into overdrive.
The auxiliary's
activity of the spirit.
The chalice overflowed.

The moon enormous on the harbour,
I could drive into it,
pushed by the white line streaming past
while cormorants tuck into their wings and sleep.

The world is fleshed with dark.
The earth drinks me greedily.
Come home, it says,
Go back to her.

II. *Waiting Here*

This is not my room.
It's quiet, cool.
The cat has more right to be here.

The scotch is waiting.
Also the ice.
You haven't come home yet
but your smell remains from morning.

The bed's been made.
The place seems untenanted.
As if you were waiting for a
candidate from the day's heat.

Why expect the walls to beat like a heart
bringing you back?
On a small pad
this writing's squeezed.

Now the cat has gone,
its place taken by the ticking minutes.
I would have been more at home
to have passed through the open window,

come to beg at the spread table.

III. *The Misty Heart*

Through the clouds of bedclothes
comes your face, a misty heart.
What beats with it
not the shallow muscle in my chest
but another deep within,
a tiny pulsing heart.

So the moon embraces night, her brother,
drained and sick of himself.
She has taken his strength from the day,
the moon in gauze,
now veils herself in white.

Odd that in this darkness
I should feel the white of your arms
as pink suffuses through your face.
Odd you should be living here with me.

THE SAXOPHONE TO ITS SAXOPHONIST

Take my adder's head into your mouth
and let the reed speak its name.
We're together in the blare, locked
coiled fingers on bright metal.
Dip with me into the brassy glow, sobbing,
no longer instrumentalist,
you are the instrument. Your lungs
my womb, your lips my opening.
The rigid heating bud grows, swells, plunges
in the dwelling place of air,
we've peopled it.
Your slightest breath is my tonight.
The throbbing bell
swings in the gap of the world
made word made sound, my beak
nods, swivels, nudges, swerves
healing the wound and feeding it,
brings it home, relieved and happy.
We weep while others drink,
fill their glasses with our tears.
I have the snakehead's love,
kissing its own poison.
I am X. Crossroads
blitz the register, fingerpulse on molten pennies
blasting through the broken bottle night.
What you want you need.
You must shape your smile into a grimace,
your cheek's a cherub's, while I take you down
cellar into darkness, into dawn
shine song, swooping
smoky lust, far into our hazy secret dream.
Where the snake swallows its tail
I'll be richer for your dying wish,
your glad fist at my throat.

THE ABSENT FATHER

Now that he's no longer here
there's no call for continuance of anger
or continuance at all. What falls away
is always. All days have him now.

At leisure I may invent
the seven deadly sins for him.
Sum up, subtract from someone
only himself, perishable quantity.

Because we could never hear his mind,
his body became of it.
We read him like a barometer,
tapping to make sure.

Sometimes he talked to himself,
plodding toward the filled house
then cornered by the window.
His pipe held the scripture of the dark.

He was unequal to his pleasures,
ample to his pain.
The reins he gripped like an epitaph,
six wild horses couldn't pull him down.

But why invest the past,
except the past alone has surety?
If this man was reliable
all takes on sudden risk.

GENOCIDE

They did not always paint memorably, or play concerti
on patiently restored instruments of the 18th century,
nor did they write acceptably universal humanistic novels,
or devote themselves to scientific research for mankind's benefit.
Some of them, let us admit, would normally be locked away,
certified as deranged, retarded, or merely criminal.
Some were inclined to cheat you on the purchase of a bedroom
     suite,
in a railway station your pockets would not be safe from them.
Some had warts, pimples, betrayed unpleasing body odours,
carried and spread the less condonable social diseases,
slobbered, gawked, picked their noses and sampled the harvest.
Some were not particularly articulate—loud, gauche, ignorant,
even frankly bigoted. Some were simply boring.

Nor, if we look at other continents, may we assume
they always lived exemplary tribal lives of natural simplicity,
or tolerated those who threatened traditional hunting ground.
They failed to observe standards of civilized warfare we expect.
In some districts, torture or slavery was not unknown.
Every now and then they ate their prisoners.
On occasion, they abandoned elders or exposed unwanted young.
Standards of hygiene and personal care fell often short.
They distended upper lips with plugs, sliced off labia.
In many ways they earned our disapproval,
just as far away in cities, others got conspicuously bad grades
from you or I or whoever scores the tests.
Like the beautiful, the kind, the talented, they too were butchered.

SHE IS ALL GONE INTO THE WORLD OF LIGHT

Mystic tunes, guru times, mantra messages,
Indian passages, pinks and blues and mauves.
The archetype of the Wise Old Man
draws her close to the framed photograph
of the holy in-touch greybeard,
incense and candles. We her betrayers
slink around or skulk in corners,
sneering, cynical, muttering "deluded."
She floats to the door, disembodied.
Soon we will only have her astral body
to look at for foreignness, and she
will have shucked off illusion in a distant house
on the slope of green hills, at peace, zones
beyond us, glad to be off the wheel.
She will take instruction
in how to be part of all herself, the One
welcoming her: "What took you so long?"

LIGHTED WINDOWS

Behind the dense film of curtains
the man and the woman supposedly
his wife move, barrel-bodied, to their beds
not locatable by me.
Perhaps I hope they'll disclose
some erotic act, in stolid middle age
engage in a slow revelation,
shedding poundage, years, and sweat.
Now they glide in dream-fed concentration,
mine or theirs I do not know,
and though I am intent on what seems to be
the nocturnal domestic shuffle,
if we met on the daylit sidewalk.
I would not recognize them,
but then again there is no sign
I do so now. Her hair seems bound
by a net, a bulbous shadow.
Are they quarrelling, or have they lapsed
into a long-summoned sullenness
as a question summons a reply
until their room, window, my balcony backyard
are filled with the implacable destiny of answers?

THE HISTORY OF MODERN EUROPEAN POETRY

I am heartily tired of them, these European poets,
their quest for absolutes, their pure intentions
lines packed with content ethical, aesthetic
symbolic, metaphysical. Though elsewhere others suffer
nowhere such refinement of suffering,
degradation, indigence. Syphilis, dope, dipsomania,
emblems of their medieval guilds. Weary
of warfront suicides, gulags, and internment camps,
entire countries devoured by hungry isms and ologies.
The catastrophic loves, the early incest, the
last this, the final that, their
inclusive languages, how silence is statement, how
impurity is programmatic. Dismayed
by such intelligence, stamina, and diary-keeping,
tuberculosis, orphanhood. How much better to be in America
where with virile voices we
yodel ditties in the slipstream of our own wind.

THE ELF-DOLL

For my son of 30 months, my mother
has produced this relic of my childhood
an elf-doll, its face a cherub's
in hard glazed plastic,
huge blue eyes and painted lashes
the rest stuffed wool in Santa colours
now grubby. She tells us it
belonged to my brother,

five years older, spastic from birth,
dead at 21. I cannot connect
this blonde, radiant boy and the
instrument of his delight with
the other boy

held wrenched over the toilet seat,
whose teeth rotted and fell out,
whose every meal was a howl,
whose waking and falling asleep were howls, differently pitched
who died with drowning lungs,
whose lashes were long, whose eyes were dark.

He cuddles it, and calls it his baby.

LOOKING AWAY

When we talk you'll notice
I do not look directly
at you but downward or ahead, my good ear
inclined toward your words, now
and then glancing briefly at you to affirm
I am still listening, still there.
If I should look into your eyes
the chances are I am bored or indifferent,
my face a mask and not an ear,
but looking away I am looking into
what you will say next.
At this moment you may be sure
I am with you and that I find
the truth a foot in front of me,
two feet from you.

THE DAY THE SUMMER ENDED

was sunny warm on the lakeside beach.
The two girls bent toward the seagull,
their hair blonde brown, the long slope of
their backs and legs,
vertical muscles of their flanks,
intent on the seabird
that blinked and was it wounded,
rabid, why couldn't it fly?
They flexed ankles at it, they made a pass of hands,
picked it up, set it down.
Still it stood all but motionless
on the grimy sand. Then an older man
in beachwear strolled toward them smiling.
He crouched to take a photograph
of the girls stroking the feathered creature
and the trio ambled away chatting,
sun in their eyes.

A MEMORIAL

Half-deaf, I sit in the back row
half-listening as
readers mumble into the mike
words by or about the dead writer
Once in a while there's a chuckle
sundered laughter, broken applause
something funny must have been said
but the event's joyless, griefless
as if no one had much liked this sour
chronically depressed individual
nor ever met his work with rage or elation.
I gave him a bad review, he gave me one,
we're even.
This dutiful tribute's sleepwalked through,
months after the demise,
class loyalty,
useless thanks to one who'd
toiled in a stony field.
The librarian M.C.'s gracious enough
but there's no food or drink
and the stacked books on the back table,
most by one of the readers,
mostly go unsold, we glumly scatter
Where were the others, the man's family?
Did he have a family?
Or was perpetual disgrace his stock in trade?
What has gone before? The passion of regret?
A jig around a wakeful casket?
What lives on after?
Scribere est agere
but to not write is also to act.
With barbiturates and a plastic bag
he achieved silence.

BREAKUP

The final signal was when they took the bed away.
Mattresses, headboards, floorboards slump in the box
and V. hops in the cab with a tall dark stranger.
Sprouting in the sodden November leaves
the lawn sign says Village Realty, make us an offer.
For months now the couple had followed a new rotation.
V. there weekdays with the two kids, B. on weekends.
Where do they sleep together or apart?

We doors away have tried to splice spotty information.
seeking when or what went wrong. Was it midsummer
when despite B.'s vasectomy V. got pregnant, got rid of it?
Did B., raised Catholic, resent this? Or we speculate
maybe V. wanted to be talked out of it and the lapsed B.
decided that would betray his hardwon lack of faith.
Maybe it was a mutual decision to nix an inconvenience.
Maybe, this is going too far, the baby wasn't his?

Up to then they seemed fine, just another
boomer couple on a family street V. anxious because
our kid supposed to pick up their kid after school,
gets his wires crossed and she doesn't know where her kid is.
But he went home with another kid, that's all right.
B., lean and weedy in rumpled bathrobe, offers me a beer,
at night sits on the steps with his son spotting planes.
Which take off land, land take off?

No doubt about the weekend the crisis hit B. didn't come home.
A furious V., her face a mess, aimed to see
a legal aid lawyer, we invited her to dinner to talk it out,
maybe we could help arrange a baby-sitter but
then she cancelled. B. returned and we didn't hear more,
assumed they'd worked it out, it's their business. If
a marriage's shot down should we locate, decode the black box,
decide which pilot mistook a mountain for a cloud?

We notice V.'s wardrobe, how shopbound she used to strut
in tight ditzy pants, bright patchwork jacket, cute peaked cap,
ripe and jaunty, but now subdues herself in sombre hues.
All this is sad, but of course the saddest business is the kids,
a boy for B., a girl for V. The girl's too young to know
what's really going on, the boy knows they're going to move,
maybe that his dad won't take him and our kid to McDonald's
anymore. Has he got more to go on than that?

I think back to the spring. With help and plans B.
had hammered and slotted together a hardwood deck
overlooking their backyard, crisscrossed with lines and toys.
He was proud of it, that deck. What better symbol
to show a brave resolve to mend the things gone wrong?
At that point had they even gone wrong? Or the story
takes another tilt—was the deck's assertion a false spring?
Who knows the secrets of the human hearth?

MY FATHER TALKS TO HIMSELF

My father, eight years dead, comes up the walk,
talking to himself. He likes to talk to
an intelligent man and
he likes to hear an intelligent man talk.
We cannot hear what he's saying,
he's the only one who can hear him.

We cannot hear what he's saying but
his hearing has always been excellent.
He walks and talks confirming
what he's said all along,
the sum of his additions:
one plus one equals one.

We too have done our accounting:
a word here, a word there,
each telling as prayer,
read silence between footfalls as
his pronounced opinions
close on the house

but his manners are good:
he does not speak unless spoken to.
Steps have custody of speech,
to be candid is to be misunderstood,
to talk and walk the safe and only time
he says and does together.

This morning he shakes his head down,
accusing his addresses,
who or what reminds and reproaches,
or enabled might
add denials he's done already,
and still he stays on his path,

well-beaten pathways of his brain
swaying on their stem.
He ambles into our lives, we who
live inside the house, outside him, we
who cannot hear him, never have or will
now he's dead.

ABDALS*

Where they cross the street,
what they eat for breakfast,
seems to be significant
but they don't know why
nor how it should be that
families and friends seem strangers
while they belong to a sodality
whose rules are unwritten, unspoken,
secret sharers of provided-for benevolence.

They sense that they are placed
to do something sublimely important
but the drag of moment to moment
belies this ostensibly.
Even so the uncanny feeling persists
that their slightest motions direct continuance,
of the world even.

Since this doesn't seem sensible
they dismiss it as an idle thought.
Yet they intuit that when they die
this work, whatever it is,
will be carried on by someone else.

Each night before they sleep
they take a certain puzzled satisfaction
that what they did has counted in some way.

*Abdals. The name given by Moslems to certain mysterious persons whose identity is known only to God and through whom the world is able to continue its existence. When one dies another is secretly appointed to fill the vacant place. *Brewer's Dictionary of Phrase & Fable.*

CATS & SQUIRRELS & DOGS & JUNG

The dialectic's simple enough.
Cats will attempt to kill squirrels.
Squirrels win by not being killed,
heap and drop payloads of squirrility
on pard-won battle ribbons.
But a dog interferes, wish matched with incompetence,
maybe killer of squirrels and cats but who knows
what's in the flyspecked cross-hairs of a dog:
the random factor, fog spoiling the dawn assault,
a field marshal down with gastro-enteritis,
treads shredding off the lead tank, some vital message
arriving too late or scrambled in transit.
Dogs' warp and woof skew best-effort calculations
of vertical takeoff and trajectory. Cats
are precisians given muddy pause by complexity,
theorems shot to hell, the pure Euclidean
twisted by loopy quantums. Squirrels
might welcome barking mad distractions
but like cats they believe in rules and now
the game spirals out of control as the flanneled oaf
blunders onto the playing fields of Eton.
The feline rodent struggle so strangely restful,
almost serene, is queered by chance. A dog is god.

BECKET

After the barons hacked Becket to death
their clerk set his foot on the dead man's neck
and with his sword point scattered
his brains on the floor, exclaiming "This traitor
will not rise again."

Later, monks see the martyr's hairshirt,
drawers sewn tightly round his trunk and thighs
which could nonetheless be opened at the back
for the daily scourging. The garments
are alive with vermin.

The vermin alive, and Becket dead.
Alive, Becket inviting filth
to feast on his goodness, giving it
a home his discomfort their comfort.
He was one, they were many,
now he is none: they multiply.

Before monks' eyes minute connections swarm.

MODEL

On its mile of track on a scale of 1/48
the Model Railroad Club of Toronto
is showing how the province or at least the country
or at least the world
should be run.

Beside their trains engineers sedately glide
keeping time, and in his booth above
the dispatcher sets the clock.

From busy Lilleyburg,
railyard southern terminus,
steam or diesel trains
travel down the valley,
cross creeks and rivers, loop and disappear
into a tunnel, scoot across
a suspension bridge
northbound
to Ebertville.

Main line to branch line,
mine to feed mill,
sawmill to dock.
A lake freighter rides an unruffled surface,
tourists inspect a quarry,
old cannery, new restaurant—
all is industry
never idle, ever productive,

and though the Central Ontario Railway
is near perfection much
remains to be done.

In this former munitions plant
modellers do piece-work,
tracks and sidings, a steeldeck bridge,
more switches and scenery,

new paint factory, coal trestle, another paper mill.
An unseen hand carves the rockface,
lays the bed.

There is rest in such activity.
The world would be a better place if
the Model Railroad Club of Toronto were running it.
Any train is walking distance
and a trip takes 15 minutes.

JANICE, PATSY, DAISY

It must have been painfully obvious to my father
that I would never be a farmer.
For one thing, I was too smart.

Nonetheless, I joined 4-H and pledged
        My Head to clearer thinking
        My Heart to greater loyalty
        My Hands to larger service
        and my Health to better living
For my club, my community, and my country.

I learned to judge mature Jersey cows in milk,
pinbones to hookbones, heart girth, spring of rib,
        General Appearance
        Mammary System
        Dairy Character
        Capacity

and though a shapely parade passed my critical eye
I remember best the purebred calves
my father bought for me.

Janice, Patsy, Daisy

Angular Janice with her long, shrewd face,
her fawn coat, gentle on the halter,
but with her sisters given to savage hooks
with her curved horns, grown to a no-nonsense cow
of power and authority, a born leader.

Patsy, my last, the sweet and dark,
her doe eyes and silken muzzle,
her deep-dished head on whose brink
bloomed tender buds, whose soft steps
led me around the ring.

And Daisy, also dark, the immature teats
below her body's swell, as
calf, yearling, two-year-old my champion,
whose hooves I lavished with neat's-foot-oil,
whose svelte haunches I brushed but won,
for herself alone, and not because of me.

I think now of their beauty
and that they are dead.
Janice, Patsy, Daisy.

PEOPLE AND THE WEATHER

This is after all what's left,
people and the weather.
Who died.
Who was born
of which parents down the road.
That she almost didn't make it
to the hospital, what nurses she had.
Or perhaps it was the driving rainstorm
the day of the funeral,
only a back braced to the wind
and someone being buried
or rain falling, casting ground
into footsteps of eternity.
The next day. Sunlight. So hot
not a damn thing will grow.
Thus people count their blessings.
No, it's like this: the people
are neighbours and have their doings
as we do and the weather, well
it's always there, to be noted
as yesterday's, today's, tomorrow's.
The weatherman, one of the local gods.
The weatherman said
and he was wrong or he was right.
Here comes the snow, ice on the highway,
a person skids, they always
drank too much, the whole family.
A list of names is enough,
a recital of temperatures,
hell to pay if we don't get rain,
a shower for the bride.

MY ROOM AT THE ST. CHARLES

I'm on the third. The guy on the second
tells me one night going to bed he heard
a low humming he couldn't place. Arising
he located it outside his door. There
sprawled on the floor was a woman
rolling cigarettes. She looked up and said
"Want some company?" I'm in 326. Last
Saturday someone leaped from 318, he'd
been there two years. The police were a while
piecing together the note he left, glass
from his window crunched underfoot for days.
The ground-floor barkeep
said the man broke his spine in two places
and complained about the pain.
All day he'd been behaving strangely,
running up and down the stairs.
                                        At night
I look around my room, at the pitted desk,
the stained carpet, the dinged chair, the chipped walls,
            and it seems to me
that these people live in rooms like mine.
So whenever I want to collapse on the floor,
pleading for company, when I look the long way down
and feel like jumping I stop and think:
            You don't have to.
                        It's been done before.
This for some reason gives me hope.

MYSELF & NAPOLEON BONAPARTE

Napoleon was born in Ajaccio.
I in Pictou.

His family was long established in Corsica.
Mine in Nova Scotia.

Napoleon's schoolmates made fun of how he talked.
My schoolmates called me Elmer Fudd.

Napoleon went to École Militaire in Brienne,
I to West Pictou District High School in Lyons Brook.

He repressed an uprising in the Vendée on 13 Vendemaire.
I threw a Coke bottle at a fellow fan at a football game.

Napoleon married Marie Rose Josephine Tascher de la Pagerie.
I married Laura Alison Millicent Armour.

His son was born in the Tulieries.
Mine in Women's College Hospital.

Napoleon named a Marshal's wife Duchess of Dantzig.
We named our standard poodle Darcy.

The *Northumberland* bore Napoleon to the island of St. Helena.
I lived near Northumberland Strait and Prince Edward Island.

In exile Napoleon lived on what had been a farm.
So did I.

At the end of his life Napoleon may have been poisoned.
In adolescence I suffered from stomach pains.

Most of Napoleon rests in the Invalides.
My body parts will go to invalids.

THE OFFICE

is all it is,
bare walls, a folding bed,
white-lacquer desk,
papers, books, typed pages.
From the door one's eyes move
in a swift diagonal
toward the bathroom, edge of bath
in which the writer often steeps,
toilet on which he squats.

The inner voice spoke
in the silence words,
illimitable whisper,
but the neighbour's dog
drove him crazed
with its yapping,
nothing in the universe but
music and noise
but you couldn't hear the music
for the ragged barking thing

he found one morning feeding on garbage
in the alley, living only to bark,
shit, chafe its chain,
and so the writer took a rope,
tied it round the neck of noise,
dragged it into the bathroom,
and hacked it to death.

"Let me show you the mark," he said,
"where I missed with the hatchet."
You can see the chip,

the chip in the enamel.

BETHEL CAROL SERVICE

Again we are summoned here to sameness
in Sunday suits, dragged shuffling to our feet,
mumbling with the choir somewhat swelled for the occasion,
who show the usual strain struggling by rote
through "Little Town of Bethlehem" and "Silent Night."
Dense in pews we still have to look at the hymn book.
We glance up to see the stumble to the front
of shepherds and wise men round yon virgin,
and the infant of course, sometimes live, this year stuffed.
The scripture comes wreathed out of close air,
stale as the cramped slow wings of angels.
At last comes that crowd-pleaser "Joy to the World."
What joy in this world? Where is the red gold glory,
the sky parting, a knowing that the world has changed
today, always, and forever? We had managed a few wan smiles at
the littlest angels and cute sheep, now in the basement
stiffly stand at the back to make a muster of grins
as Santa Claus, the junior god, disburses candy.
Outside we exchange a few crisp nods in the snow-flecked air,
then go veering and swerving home
on the clogged icy roads. It's over for another year,
while somewhere, sometime, somehow long ago
He of the thousand names and power unimaginable
came down to live with people just as dull as us.

BOXING DAY PARTY

After the turkey comes The Adjective Game.
Adjectives will be slotted into
blanks in a prepared script, each paired
with the name of someone in the family.
The regretted absent will receive a copy later.
So, crowded in the living-room, one by one we provide
(the littlest need prompting) adjectives
till all the blanks are filled by a tall thin man
who then reads aloud our story. To laughter,
sometimes forced, we hear of the *pompous* W, the *nubile* X,
the *antediluvian* Y, the *rigid* Z, or as
it may be the *erudite* W, the *adamant* X,
the *Machiavellian* Y, the *winsome* Z. All
are us, all the above is true, ah,
we cannot tell since this is a family,
dissolving in blood the true or false,
blood bound with others, family overarching all.
But how long can we persist in being family?
When do degrees of separation part us as
matriarchs and patriarchs fade or vanish
and the others age, procreate, grow, or marry?
How long before we find ourselves in a
strange living-room surrounded by unfamiliars
and why am I here and what was your name again?
Yet for decades we have played The Adjective Game,
plucking from the random air exactly who we are.

CAFÉ ISTANBUL

Seen through the window
smoking, drinking, womanless,
they are doomed men.

I don't know what they do in there
or I do: the slap of cards,
the crash of dominoes.

The street has nothing to do with them,
doubly separate.
The flag on the wall has something.

They will probably go home at some point
but they may spend
the rest of their lives here,

earnestly melancholy,
knowing each other.

A DRIVE IN THE RAIN

In the dry summer they say it is the rain has fallen
on us equally and well, and we only want to drive
stopping and going, as the rain stops and goes
about its falling business. The wheels hum
when they don't bump into the pits and pocks
of this grey paved road curving to the sea.
We have left a tall house whose lean boards drank
under the dripping leaves. It was a loan
and this time is lent us, too, a present wrapped
by the many-fingered rain. Over a crest
the slant to the strait. Now we are hugging
mud flats and tidal pools of an undemanding shore,
bending round one province to another.
Birds, dippers of air, don't mind the wet,
in fact, they seem to like it.
We get out to walk below their flight
where at the edge of green it's our own envelope,
this damp quotient of happiness.

INDEX OF POEMS

Many of the poems in this book appeared, though not necessarily for the
first time, in the following collections:

Green. **PAW**

Here. **WF**

History of Modern European Poetry, The. The *Idler* 24 (July & August 1989)

In the White Morning. The *Idler* 4 (April/May 1985)

In the Provinces. **MW**

Janice, Patsy, Daisy. **PAW**

Leamington Cemetery. **WF**

Lighted Windows. **WF**

Looking Away. The *Idler* 19 (September & October 1988)

Loving. The *Tamarack Review* 70 (1977)

Madwomen. Dreadnaught Press, 52 Pickup series; **WTW**

Man Who Heard Symphonies, The. *Nebula* 13 (1980)

Matushka Case, The. *Northern Journey* 1 (1971)

Memorial, A. Letters Bookshop, Twobitter Bit Poetry series No. 58 (1994)

Model. **PAW**

My Father Talks to Himself. **PAW**

My Room at the St. Charles. **PAW**

Myself & Napoleon Bonaparte. **PAW**

Now is the Time to Hold Her Close and Tell Her You Love Her. *Nebula* 13 (1980)

Office, The. **PAW**

Old N.S.. **MW**

On Foreign Women. **WTW**

Only My Typewriter. **MW**

People and the Weather. **PAW**

Phoning. In *Storm Warning* 2. Ed. Al Purdy, (1976)

Piazza, The. *Impulse* 2, No.1 (Autumn 1972)

Return to Cold Comfort Farm. *Pottersfield Portfolio* 1 (1979-80)

Saxophone to Its Saxophonist, The. **WF**

Self-Consumed. **WF**

She is All Gone into the World of Light. **WF**

Siren. *Light in Darkness*, (1973)

Sofian Episode. The *Tamarack Review* 58 (1971)

Some Cases in Point. The Word Bookshop, Chough Series, (1977)

Three Feminine Fantasies. **WF**

Traces. **MW**

Train Moving, The. *Northern Journey* 1 (1971)

Upstairs Window. *Quarry*, (Autumn 1972)

Visages dans la rue. **MW**

Whitefaces. In *Un Dozen*. Ed. Judith Fitzgerald

With the Dog. The *Grad Post*, 3, No. 8 (11 Dec. 1975)